GT40

THE LEGEND LIVES ON

GT40
THE LEGEND LIVES ON

JOHN S. ALLEN

First published in Great Britain in 1995
by Osprey, Michelin House,
81 Fulham Road, London SW3 6RB

ISBN 185532 524 1

Project Editor Shaun Barrington
Editor Jane Northey
Page design Paul Kime
Printed in Hong Kong

Dedication

To the memory of Ken Wells – a true race car enthusiast if ever there was one.

Acknowledgements

Without the help of many people, this book would not have been possible. My thanks go to Henri Bercher, Dave Cundy, Georges Filliez, Lee Holman, Robert Horne, Don Hume, Roger Jaynes, Gary Kohs, Rod Leach, Pete Lyons, Charles Ordowski, Ronnie Spain, Jim Stanton, George Stauffer, Jürgen Strehle, Peter Thorpe, Bryan Wingfield, The Ford Motor Company, PR staff at Lime Rock Park, Road America and Silverstone, and the owners of the many cars featured in this book. Thank-you also to Shaun Barrington and the staff at Osprey, for making the production of this book a pleasure.

Front cover

The one and only all-American Le Mans winner on one of its very rare forays away from the enormous halls of the magnificent Henry Ford Museum. Dan Gurney and AJ Foyt drove this Shelby American Ford Mark IV to a record-breaking win at Le Mans in 1967. It could be argued that, in the strictest sense, this car is not a GT40 at all, but is just a "Mark IV", but the term GT40 has become a generic title for all of Ford's sport-racing cars of the mid-sixties.

Back cover

A colourful pack of GT40s snapping at the heels of Road America's pace car as they head towards the grid for the start of the all-GT40 race which commemorated the marque's thirtieth birthday. (Photo: Pete Lyons)

Title page

GT40P/1026 displays its beautiful Essex Wire livery, which included two triangular matt black panels on the front bonnet. These were intended to reduce the glare which would otherwise come from stark white body panels, and which would dazzle the driver.

For a catalogue of all books published by Osprey Automotive please write to:

The Marketing Department,
1st Floor, Michelin House, 81 Fulham Road, London SW3 6RB

About the Author

John S. Allen is a Chartered Accountant who regrets that adding up columns of figures must all too often take priority over photographing GT40s, Porsche 962s and other fine sports-racing cars and Fords. He lives in the dismal Northern wastelands known as West (or Wet) Yorkshire, England, where motor sport is all but extinct, and shares his home with his wife Jennifer, a Mustang called Henry, and a Capri called The Capri.

Introduction

At times it is hard to believe that the Ford GT40 has been around for more than thirty years; indeed, it seems like only a moment ago that it was at Watkins Glen for a big party to celebrate its 25th birthday. The mystique surrounding the GT40 does not diminish with time, but rather it grows, as present-day trends lead us to look back ever more fondly on the days when GT40s were state-of-the-art racing cars, competing at the very highest levels in the most gruelling endurance races around the world. Thankfully, there are still a lot of GT40s around, most of them having survived the rigours of thousands of miles of cut and thrust competition.

GT40 enthusiasts have something else to be thankful for. Whilst a gathering of cars from the GT40's old adversary, Ferrari, can produce a host of beautiful machines, they have a certain redness which can soon prove to be a trifle boring; not so with the GT40, where national colours were abandoned long ago, and reds were joined by blues, black, silver, gold, green, white, yellow…In the days before racing cars became mobile billboards was there ever a racer as colourful as the GT40? Just look at the photographs, dream a little, then start to plan your visit to the next anniversary gathering!

Below

The controversial dead heat which earned 1046 its place in the history books now far behind, 1046 is seen here in Road America's officials' car park, towing-harness in place for the trip back to the paddock. Note the classic Mark II-A features: air scoops, Halibrands, raised front fenders, fully-ducted spare-wheel cover, and quick-lift jacking points.

Contents

Below

Ex-Ford France GT40, 1003; the first of the production batch to take part in an endurance race, with Guy Ligier and Maurice Trintagnant at the Nürburgring 1000km, 23 May, 1965. Apart from the new licence number, (originally JBH 373C), the car looks just as it did when racing in its second season, 1966. (Photo: Robert Horne)

A Never-ending Story

From July 22 to July 24, 1994, there unfolded the latest chapter in the story of the GT40. The venue was Elkhart Lake's Road America, and the occasion was the International 30 Year GT40 Reunion, organised by George Stauffer, of Wisconsin-based Stauffer Classics Inc. The reunion was held in conjunction with the annual Chicago Historics race meeting, featuring the Como Inns-sponsored International Challenge.

Thirty years... it didn't seem that long ago that Ford's space-age sports racer made its public debut at the New York Auto Show. The first of the Ford GTs, a sleek white and blue, low-slung coupe, stunned the automotive world, not merely by its dramatic appearance, but also by its stated purpose – to win Le Mans, a feat never before achieved by a large-volume car manufacturer.

Ford had tried to buy Ferrari and had failed. Negotiations had been going well, and signatures on paper were but a whisker away, when realisation dawned on the aging Enzo Ferrari: he would no longer be The Boss. He wanted to sell his company, but continue to run it, and under Ford auspices that could not be. The briefcases were closed, the hotels vacated, and the Ford negotiating team left Modena, never to return.

Over thirty years later, we can be thankful for the

old man's fearfulness. His rejection of Ford's advances led Henry Ford II to decree that Ford would go it alone in sports car racing, and would beat the Ferraris which they could not join. The result was the Ford GT, an extraordinary combination of American money and direction, British race car design, and hardware sourced from whatever country could supply it.

Never before had Ford attempted anything even remotely like the GT project, and it was inevitable that their path would not be an easy one. One of their first decisions was that the GT would be built not by the main Ford company, but by a self-contained offshoot which would not be bound by the mass of red tape and bureaucracy which afflicts all large corporations. The system worked and, under the watchful eyes of Roy Lunn, John Wyer and Eric Broadley, the Lola-inspired Ford GT took shape in Lola's Slough workshops.

Its track debut was not auspicious. When tested in the wind-tunnel, the car's shape had proved to be of admirably low drag, but since nobody had actually given any thought to the problem of lift versus drag, it is now, with hindsight, no surprise that lift was present in abundance. Ford quickly learned that there was more to race-car design than merely using computer-generated results; if the computers weren't asked the right questions, they could hardly be blamed for not giving the right answers. Initially the outcome was an unstable car whose pretty shape had the aerodynamic qualities of a wing, and which would happily fly when speeds of 200mph were attained; the Le Mans tests provided two wrecked cars, some hurt

Drivers: Denny Hulme
Richard Piper
Herve Regout
M. Weidenbusch

Above

Precursor of the Ford GT was the Lola Mk6 GT, two of the three examples built being acquired by Ford to act as development mules for the new Ford. The third Lola went to John Mecom's team, and was Chevrolet-powered. Now part of the Peter Kaus Rosso-Bianco collection, it is seen here at the Nürburgring. The similarity in overall layout between the Lola and the Ford which followed it is obvious.
(Photo: Jürgen Strehle)

pride, and a lesson learned. Ford really did learn those lessons, but it took a long time to get everything right. The entire four-year GT project cost many millions of dollars, but provided Ford with a wealth of knowledge and experience. The 1964 season was a dismal one, as the steep learning curve was climbed ever higher, seemingly with the peak never reached. When the whole racing (as opposed to manufacturing) part of the project was handed

and 1965 seasons could be at Road America for the 30 year reunion. One of the duo was actually but a stone's throw away, just north of Chicago. GT/104 survived a fire and explosion at Le Mans in 1964, finished third at Daytona in 1965, and provided an epic drive at the Nürburgring, recovering from 23rd position to 8th after running out of fuel just short of the pits. Alas, its painstakingly accurate restoration, during which some of Daytona's sand had been discovered in the innermost reaches of its chassis, had not been completed in time for the gathering.

Already there is talk of another reunion, perhaps in 1996, to celebrate thirty years of the most important achievement of all: winning at Le Mans. The 1966 season saw a significant change of direction, as experience showed that the pair of 7-litre prototypes which had run at Le Mans in 1965 were definitely the way to go, despite some – notably John Wyer – arguing that it's cars, not engines, that win races.

1966 was the Year of the Mark II – winner at Daytona, Sebring (in open-topped X-1 guise) and Le Mans. The X-1 was chopped up many years ago, but many of the other Mark IIs were present at Road America. Pride of place just had to go to GT40P/1046, the black and silver Mark II which took top honours at Le Mans. But who could look at the beautiful 1015, winner at Daytona, without feeling some sadness? Wearing its Le Mans livery, the Daytona victory was not even hinted at; many believe that 1015 should have been the Le Mans winner and, had politics not intervened, it would have been. It would also have given Ken Miles a unique treble – victory at the one 12-hour and both 24-hour races in one season. Miles's death at Riverside in August 1966 made 1015's appearance all the more poignant.

Elkhart Lake saw all three of the 1966 Le Mans finishers gathered together, to celebrate first, second and third places, in arguably Ford's finest competition hour (although fans of open-wheelers may claim otherwise).

Another famous winner was present at Road America – the Mark IV which opened Ford's score-

over to Shelby American, the results at first took a dramatic turn for the better, but the excellent placings at Daytona and Sebring, the first two long distance races of the 1965 season, were not to be matched during the remainder of a disappointing year which saw the GT displaying speed aplenty, but with reliability almost non-existent.

It was a pity that neither of the two cars which shouldered most of the burden throughout the 1964

Left

The two Mark IIs which formed the controversial dead heat at Le Mans in 1966 were together again at Road America. George Stauffer owns black 1046, which was given the decision by 20 metres, ahead of Brian Mimaki's blue 1015.

card for 1967, by winning the Sebring 12 hours. 1967 was the year when Ford made another change of direction. Retaining the engine and transmission of the Mark II, an otherwise completely new car was built. Developed from the J-car which in 1966 had seen only test mileage, the Mark IV was a wholly American project which applied some new aerodynamic lessons, most importantly the use of a much slimmer cockpit, the smaller dimensions becoming available courtesy of changes in the FIA's Appendix J rules. The Mark IV also used a radically different chassis, constructed from honeycomb aluminium, and substantially lighter than its sheet-steel forebears.

1967 was another good year for the big Fords, and for most of the time the disasters of the early days could be forgotten. An unfortunate hiccough at Daytona, where all the Mark IIs succumbed to transmission problems caused by faulty heat-treatment of gearbox shafts, was followed by the Sebring win, already mentioned, and another victory at Le Mans.

The 1967 Le Mans win was less clear-cut than in the previous year. Whilst a 1-2-3 looked at one time to be on the cards, a stroke of appalling luck prevented it, and put Ford in the position of having to defend its position with great care. A single accident, caused by brake pads being incorrectly fitted to Mario Andretti's Mark IV during a pit stop, resulted in three Fords being wiped out.

Only two of the seven-strong Ford contingent made it to the chequered flag, but one of them was in first place, which was all that was necessary.

There has long been a question mark over the identity of the red Mark IV which took Dan Gurney and A. J. Foyt to that first-ever all-American Le Mans win. J5 or J6? The winning car shows evidence of having both numbers stamped into its aluminium tub, but, whatever number it is entitled to, there is one thing of which there is no doubt: the Henry Ford Museum's Mark IV is the Le Mans winner. Courtesy of the Museum, the most famous Mark IV of them all took its place at Road America, lining up alongside Ford's other winners.

Above

In 1966, Ford drove a coach and horses – or rather eight Mark IIs – through the convention which required race cars to carry the national colours of their manufacturers or entrants; for identification purposes, all their cars were strikingly different. How refreshing it is to see front-line racing cars unsullied by the gigantic advertisements which deface most of today's machinery; some say that it is impossible to race without commercial sponsorship, but they managed it well enough in those far off days. (Photo: Ford)

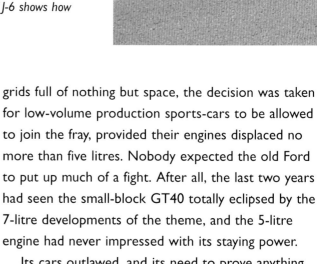

Above

Only once did the three regular Gulf GT40s, 1074, 1075 and 1076 race together, that occasion being the 1968 edition of the Le Mans 24-hours. It's a pity that nowadays all three wear the style of broad-fronted orange stripe which really is only appropriate for 1075, neither 1074 nor 1076 ever having such a paint job when they were racing back in 1968 and 1969.

Right

A memorable occasion indeed – for the first time ever, all three of Ford's Le Mans winners were together. The picture gives an ideal opportunity to compare the sleekness of the small-block Gulf car, 1075, with the muscle-bound look of its 7-litre-engined sister 1046, whilst the slimmer, more aerodynamic style of J-6 shows how trends were moving before the CSI threw a spanner in the works.

For enthusiasts everywhere but France, the changes made to the sporting regulations at the end of 1967 were a disaster. Gone were the 7-litre monsters from Ford and Chaparral, the 4-litre Ferrari 330P4s and 412Ps, the big-block Lola T70s, and the 5.7-litre Mirages. In their place came a 3-litre limit on prototypes, a limit which obviously suited the little blue cars from Matra and Alpine-Renault...

Things didn't go exactly as the legislators of the CSI had intended. Faced with the prospect of their speed-reducing engine-size limit leaving them with grids full of nothing but space, the decision was taken for low-volume production sports-cars to be allowed to join the fray, provided their engines displaced no more than five litres. Nobody expected the old Ford to put up much of a fight. After all, the last two years had seen the small-block GT40 totally eclipsed by the 7-litre developments of the theme, and the 5-litre engine had never impressed with its staying power.

Its cars outlawed, and its need to prove anything no longer there, Ford in the USA took no further part in the proceedings, other than to provide JW

Automotive Engineering with the latest go-faster (and live-longer) bits for the 289/302 inch Ford motors in the GT40. To everybody's surprise, 1968 was the GT40's Indian summer. Against all expectations, John Wyer's Gulf-sponsored GT40s won both the championship, and Le Mans. Competition came in part from Matra and Alpine, but was soon decimated; the true rival was Porsche, competing in the big league for the first time, and proving to be a force to be reckoned with. The climax of the season was Le Mans, last race in the Championship, where the Gulf GT40s

were present in comparative strength, the team numbering three cars, for the first and only time.

Those same three GT40s which raced together once only, at Le Mans 1968, were present at Road America. There was 1074, the converted Mirage, which had already had a full year's racing behind it before it began the 1968 events. 1075, the car which did most of the winning in 1968, was back in action, taking part in the GT40s-only ten lap race. There too was 1076, the youngster of the trio, which made its all too brief debut at Le Mans 1968, but had to wait

Left

The GT40 race at Road America saw 1075 starting from pole position, although the placing came from its honourable past, rather than its practice times. Alongside 1075, an empty place on the grid shows where 1046 should have been.

Top

Bob Bondurant looks happy as he poses with George Stauffer's Mark IV J-4 at the Road America reunion. Engine problems sidelined both the Mark IV and George's other 7-litre car, the Le Mans-winning Mark II, so Bob didn't get to drive in the reunion race.

Above

Viewed from the Pace Car: so many GT40s on the track together, producing a noise like rolling thunder, a spectacle of sight and sound that comes along only too rarely. (Photo: Pete Lyons)

until 1969, and a third-place finish, before it could atone for its 1968 sojourn in the Mulsanne sandbank.

1075, of course, has a special claim to fame. The surprises of 1968 were as nothing compared with the shocks of 1969. In the face of tremendous opposition from new Porsches, Ferraris and Lolas, 1075 won two of the three races in which it was entered – Sebring and Le Mans! Thus, Road America's 30 Year GT40 Reunion was particularly welcome, because, for the first time ever, Ford's winners from all those four Le Mans races were gathered together.

After 1969, GT40 race appearances were few and far between, but gatherings of the clan brought them together for friendly matches and displays. Then came vintage racing (known in Britain as "historic racing"), which gave the cars of the 'sixties another opportunity to show their paces. Vintage racing has been a major factor in keeping GT40s in good condition; scrutineering won't allow the unfit to take part.

George Stauffer and his team worked hard to ensure that the reunion was a success. Road America provided the venue for a photo-call matched only by that of the 1989 Watkins Glens meeting, and a banquet and a GT40 race provided the opportunity for old acquaintances to meet both on and off the track.

Elkhart Lake's race for GT40s was expected to be

closely fought by favourites Bob Bondurant, driving one of George Stauffer's 7-litre cars, and Brian Redman, at the wheel of GT40P/1021. Practice for the event saw both the Stauffer team's cars sidelined with engine problems, so Bondurant's plan to switch from J-4 to Le Mans winner 1046 was foiled, and his place on the grid was left unfilled.

Redman, too, had his problems. Practice revealed that 1021 was generating too much front-end lift, so canard fins were hastily manufactured and fixed to the fenders; clearly, somebody was taking this race seriously. Then came engine trouble, and Redman's race was over before it had even started. Except that

car owner Joseph Hish's chief mechanic, Jeff Sime, didn't see it that way. He refused to give up, and, instead of taking a night off and attending Saturday's banquet, he worked on, rebuilding 1021's engine so that the old car could take its place on the grid for

the start, at 1:17pm on Sunday 24 July, 1994. Forty
miles later, it was all over, and the many-times retired
Brian Redman had won yet another race in his GT40.

For Redman it was a bit like 1968, really, as experience told. His closest challenger, Don Roberts driving 1061, a 1075-clone, came home 10.175 seconds
behind Redman. Brian's average speed for the event
was 97.376mph; not at all bad for such a veteran (car,
that is).

The GT40's career as a Vintage Racer is not over
yet. GT40s have many advantages over most sports-
racing cars. They are built to be as tough as tanks,
their engines are strong (and, when broken, cheap to
replace), they're easy to maintain (try tuning an IMSA
Nissan GTP), their gearboxes are bullet-proof, and,
thanks to weight of numbers and to the Holman and
Safir projects, spares are relatively easy to obtain.

In the early part of 1994, rumours of a new Ford
high-performance car began, and in December of
that year the rumours became fact, when Ford
unveiled the GT90, their new "supercar", intended to
steal a little of the McLaren F1's thunder. The GT90's
name has links with that of the '40 but, unlike the
"40", the "90" related to the decade, not (thankfully)
to the car's height. It has been hinted that the GT90
will go into limited production, at a price which
seems dramatically low when compared with the
likes of the F1, the XJ220, the EB110 and so on. The
futuristic shape of the GT90 picks up many a styling
cue from the GT40; the GT90's front-end carrying so
many GT40-like features the old cars should feel pos-
itively flattered. Whether or not we shall see more
of the GT90 is not clear. What is clear to see is that
the GT40 legend lives on. It always will.

Right

*Perhaps only Frank Sinatra and a few heavyweight boxers have
announced their retirement more times than Brian Redman.
Mr Redman's rivals would certainly rather he switched to after-
dinner speaking (at which he is quite adept) and leave the driving to them. He's rather adept at driving, too. You can't really
argue with victory and fastest lap.*

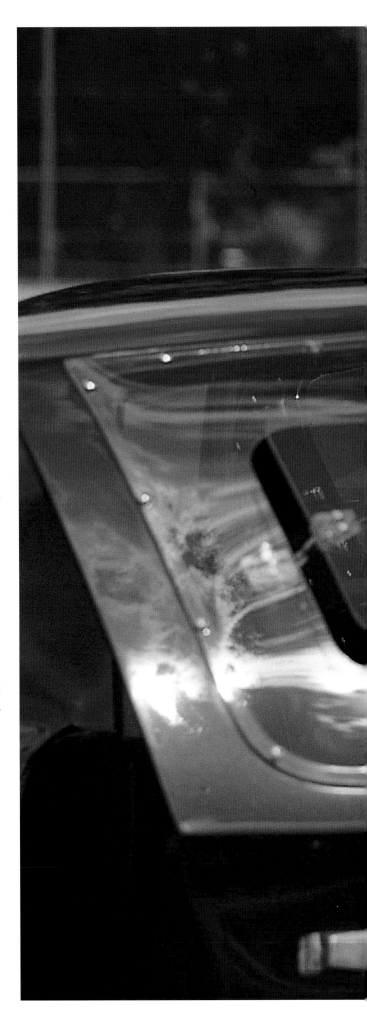

What's in a Name?

Can there be anyone, with even the most rudimentary interest in motor sport, who knows not the name GT40? Whilst that generic term has become ever more famous as the years have passed, the widely different cars which are encompassed by the name are often a source of confusion.

The Ford GT

The story of the names began in April 1964, when the first Ford GT was unveiled. Ford GT was hardly a catchy title, and it was rather misleading, in that the car was built to contest the prototype category of international sports car racing. GTs, on the other hand, (the initials stem from the European "Grand Tour" which was undertaken by wealthy socialites in the inter-war years) were essentially road-going vehicles with at least some creature-comforts, such as a

modicum of trunk space, and in racing terms they had to be built to certain minimum specified quantities.

Nonetheless, the GT part of the name stuck, and became a part of all subsequent developments of the original car. Twelve Ford GTs were built, and were numbered in series from GT/101 to GT/112. Of these twelve, the first two had a smooth nose design and a tail devoid of the transverse spoiler which was applied to all subsequent cars. Sadly, neither survives, although it is likely that parts – probably even major

Below

This rarely-seen cutaway depicts the very first version of the Ford GT. Note that across the tail there is no transverse spoiler, and above the exhausts the race number is shown painted where eventually a grille would be placed. (Photo: Ford)

parts – of their chassis were used in subsequent cars.

Before its ultimate demise, the second car, 102, was given a modified nose and tail for its outing at Le Mans in 1964, where it was joined by similarly shaped sisters 103 and 104. The same body style was used a month later, at Reims, but then that second type of nose shape was abandoned forever. It is a pity that nowadays neither of the two survivors from 1964, 103 and 104, wears its original body style.

Yet another new shape was introduced at Reims, the nose being changed again so as to allow air to pass through it more easily. The revised shape was first used on 105, another survivor which also fails to carry its original style of bodywork.

Chassis 106 was the first prototype to carry the 427 cubic inch engine, which also equipped its clone, 107, and the unique 110, the latter (known as the X-1) being a combination of Spyder bodywork and 7-litre power in an aluminium tub. Although 110 was

Above

Ford GT prototype GT/108 is currently the only intact example of the marque still to carry the correct 1965-style nose, and the low tail section unique to roadsters. 108 is the only road-ster, or "spyder", to remain in as-built condition; one survives in pieces, one was rebuilt as a coupé, one was dismantled and cut up, and one other was dismantled, probably for parts of its chassis to be incorporated in later production cars.

The very first production GT40 was GT40P/1001, seen here at the Christie's Silverstone meeting in 1991. 1001 is now in 1966 condition, restored to the livery it wore when it was loaned to the Essex Wire team for use at Le Mans, where it was driven by Jacky Ickx and Jochen Neerpasch.

indeed unique, it was nearly not so, as a second such chassis was built, but not turned into a complete car. The body style of the three 427-powered cars was different again from their predecessors, the nose being lengthened considerably in the hope of providing better penetration. Alas, it didn't. It appears that none of the three, 106, 107 and 110, survives, although the long nose from 107 still exists.

There were four other prototypes, 108, 109, 111 and 112. All were roadsters (open-topped), and all were essentially similar in shape, although the two campaigned by the British team of Ford Advanced

Vehicles had in the tops of their nose panels air-exit vents different from those equipping the two Shelby team cars. Shelby's 108 (which never raced) still exists, and is basically in original condition, an excellent example of what a 1965 Ford GT roadster should look like. Its American sister, 109, also survives, still incomplete, but slowly taking shape, albeit with a twin-cam Indy engine where a stock-block cast-iron lump should be, and with a modified nose section. It will be a happy day when the two Spyders can at last be seen together. Following an accident at the Targa Florio in 1965, 111 was chopped up, but again it seems likely that substantial parts of it were incorporated into new cars. The final roadster, 112, was rebodied as a standard GT40 coupe, and to this day remains in that form. It rarely ventures out, and for many people their only sighting of it has been the Le Mans historic event in 1973.

So it is that of all the Ford GTs, only 108 remains

in its original, as built, form. However, the other good news is that 104, which in early 1995 was nearing the end of a lengthy, major and accurate restoration, is to carry its 1965 Shelby-style bodywork, complete with all the modifications made to it when it was raced by Shelby American that year. It will thus become the only one of the original Ford GTs to be in exactly the same trim as when it was raced by one of the two works teams of the day.

The Ford GT40

The definitive name GT40 first appeared in 1965. Is there anyone who is still unaware that the "40" refers to nothing more exciting than the car's height in inches? As far as Ford was concerned, the new name applied both to the new production cars and, retrospectively, to the prototypes. The latter, following introduction of the Mark II, were renamed "Ford Mark I (GT-40)".

The GT40 was almost identical to the small-block Ford GT prototype coupes as raced by Shelby in 1965, and basically the GT40 was no more than a GT standardised for production. As with any low-volume

car, the specification actually changed rapidly, as each new racing experience taught lessons which were incorporated in cars coming down the slow assembly line. The first five examples, numbered GT40P/1001 to 1005, appeared in the period March to May 1965, and wore bodywork of the same type as had been carried by GT/105 at Rheims the previous year. The next significant change to the GT40 shape was also the last: in June 1965, GT40P/1006 received a new nose design, the so-called "Le Mans nose" (since that is where it appeared for the first time). At long last, the shape was right, and all subsequent GT40s wore that nose, or a slightly modified variant thereof. Ford GTs 103, 105, 110 and 112 also received the new

Below

The Mark IIs' bigger engine needed more air, and it was fed in by the two big scoops immediately aft of the side windows. On the rear deck two periscope-like scoops took in air for the brakes. This car is XGT-1, one of two Alan Mann-built Mark IIs which raced at Le Mans in 1966. They were substantially lighter than other Mark IIs, thanks to their use of light-alloy roof sections.

nose, and so became virtually indistinguishable from the true GT40s. By common consent, and with considerable justification, both production cars and prototypes have become known simply as GT40s, or as Mark Is.

GT40 production was numbered in the range 1001 to 1085, although there were several unnumbered chassis remaining when production ceased in 1969; these have been acknowledged as true GT40s by being allocated serials 1086 and 1108 to 1114.

One other GT40 was built well out of sequence, and given a serial number commensurate with its age. Throughout 1965 GT40P/1000 had been used as a bodywork fitting jig, not being completed in its own right until January 1966, by which time the erratic number series had reached the 1027-1036 range. 1000's first race was also its last, the car being destroyed in a tragic accident at Sebring in March 1966. Happily, most other GT40s survive, although accidents and other catastrophes have seen off 1005, 1010 (at least, the first user of that number), 1011, 1029 and 1078 (in this case also, the number's first user), whilst replacement of damaged chassis has resulted in there now being two examples each of 1009, 1012 and 1073.

During 1966 two GT40s, numbered AM.GT40.1 and AM.GT40.2, were built by Alan Mann Racing on

Above

The Mark III was an attempt to remove from the GT40 the three major shortcomings which limited its use as a road car. The headlights were raised, and made round instead of oval, to placate legislators in many US states, the tail was extended to provide at least a modicum of usable luggage space, and the gear change was made central, to permit the use of left-hand drive. Only seven Mark IIIs were built, and all still exist. This is GT40M3/1104.

chassis which had come direct to that team from chassis manufacturers Abbey Panels.

They differed from other GT40s in several ways, not the least of which was their light-alloy bodywork and superstructure. Accident damage resulted in the first of the pair being consigned to a wrecker's yard, from where it was eventually rescued. Hopefully, it will one day be rebuilt. The second is still to be seen in vintage racing.

The Ford Mark II Sports Prototype

Officially known as the Ford Mark II Sports Prototype, Mark IIs came in three different versions, and most were built on GT40 chassis, and carried chassis numbers in the GT40 series. The first two, however, were built as GT/106 and 107, and were so different from the subsequent Mark IIs that many people prefer to think of them merely as prototypes rather than as Mark IIs. Ford's retrospective allocation of the name Mark II to these two prototypes accompanied the 1966 batch of eight cars being

Left

At Watkins Glen in 1989 the only surviving Mirage M1 shows its distinctive shape. It was both lighter and more aerodynamic than the standard GT40, but problems with the CSI's rules meant that for it to supersede the GT40, at least 25 examples would have to be built. Understandably, the two Johns, Wyer and Willment, did not consider that a market existed for so many examples, and it would have been impossible for such a small operation to have completed the required number for them to have been ready for use in the 1968 season. Thus, the Mirage M1 was destined to remain a three-off car. In his superb book The Certain Sound, John Wyer tells the quaint story of the acquisition of US rights to the "Mirage" name; it's well worth reading.

renamed Mark II-A, and the 1967 rebuild of at least five of the Mark II-As as Mark II-B. In addition, three Mark II-As were built on chassis delivered direct to Alan Mann Racing; because they bypassed Ford Advanced Vehicles they did not receive chassis numbers in the GT40 series, becoming instead XGT-1 to XGT-3, but it would be pedantic in the extreme to deny them the use of the GT40 name.

Mark IIs differed from GT40s primarily in their engine (7-litres in the Mark II's case) and their gearbox, the Mark II having a Kar Kraft-built Ford T-44 4-speed in place of the GT40's ZF 5-speed.

Identification of the Mark II is made easy thanks to the car's big air-intakes sited behind the side-windows.

Throughout their racing days, Ford knew the Mark IIs as just that, and officially never credited them as being GT40s. Most Mark IIs are still with us today, although the wrecked 1011 has long since disappeared; XGT-2 has also passed out of sight, although there are not a few who suspect that it lurks behind the alias of GT40P/1009.

The Ford Mark III

Debuting in 1967, the Mark III represented Ford's final fling with the GT40 as a road-car. Although the Mark III's title did not include the GT40 epithet, all examples were built on GT40 chassis, and carried numbers in the range GT40M3/1101 to 1107, so there was no hiding their identity as GT40s. Only seven examples of the type were built, and all differed from the production GT40 in several ways, both visually and otherwise. The most obvious visual differences were quad headlights in raised fenders, and a lengthened, more nearly horizontal, tail with revised rear panel. Inside, the Mark III was unique amongst GT40s in having a central gearchange, this permitting the adoption of left-hand drive; another feature unique to the Mark III. At the time of writing all Mark IIIs still survive, and carry Mark III body-work, although it would be a relatively simple matter for an enthusiastic owner to convert them to standard GT40 specification.

The Ford Mark IV Sports Prototype

The Mark IV was the first of the Ford sports racing cars which has no claim to being a GT40, although its place in Ford's history is such that common parlance has endowed it with the GT40 title, and indeed its story is included in this publication as it is in most other books about the GT40. The Mark IV was actually a development of the Ford J-Car, a 1966 extrapolation of the Mark II, but with the most important component of all, the chassis, having almost nothing in common with its forebears.

The J-car's chassis was in honeycomb aluminium, unlike the GT40's, of sheet steel; the shape too was quite different, with totally new bodywork of (at first) aerodynamically unsound lines. For 1967 the badly shaped J-car was rebodied, and became the slippery and efficient Mark IV. Twelve J-car chassis were built, but only the first three wore J-car body-work. J-1 and J-2 no longer exist, one having been dismantled during the investigation into why the other was destroyed in a crash. J-3 was rebodied as the first Mark IV, whilst numbers 4 to 8 were built new as 1967 Mark IVs. J-9 and J-10 became Ford's Can-Am contender, the unsuccessful Ford G-7, whilst the final two, 11 and 12, remained incomplete until the mid-'eighties, when they were belatedly, and privately, completed to Mark IV specifications.

Although all the Mark IVs still survive, the J-car itself is no more, and only one G-7 (J-9) remains, the other having been apparently stolen and presumably scrapped. It is rather a pity that J-3 has never been rebodied back into its original J-car guise, for the absence of a J-car leaves a significant gap in the line-up of Ford's sports-racing hardware.

The Mirage M1

Three unnumbered GT40 chassis were taken from the production line and turned into Mirages, bearing chassis numbers M/10001 to 10003. Subsequently, with the advent of later model Mirages, none of which had even the remotest connection to the GT40, the original trio became known as Mirage M1s. The first Mirage M1 still survives in its Mirage form, the second was destroyed in a crash at the Nürburgring, and the third was rebuilt into standard GT40 specification, to become GT40P/1074.

The Mirage represented a successful attempt at improving the GT40's aerodynamics by both narrowing the cockpit, thus reducing frontal area, and refining the various air intakes and exits with which the GT40 is liberally sprinkled. Despite the car's shape being a significant improvement over that of the standard GT40, its numbers were limited to three because changes in racing regulations would have required the Mirage to be re-homologated as a production car, and there simply weren't enough customers around for the manufacture of a batch of twenty-five such cars to be a sound commercial proposition.

The GT40 Mark V

At the end of 1966, Ford Advanced Vehicles Limited ceased to be, and its assets were taken over by a new company, JW Automotive Engineering Limited, owned jointly by John Wyer and John Willment, the former providing the expertise and the latter providing most of the funding. In 1969 the new company ceased its manufacture of GT40s, and at the end of that year took on the role of Porsche's official factory team, running the awesome Gulf-backed Porsche 917Ks in international events. The day of the 917K ended with the 1971 season, and from then on the

company dabbled with mainly 3-litre DFV-powered sports cars, until eventually its racing activities were taken over by Gulf Research Racing. The company didn't die and, by then in John Willment's ownership, it diversified into other areas, including the operation of gas stations!

The company kept most of its stock of GT40 parts, and, through agents, ensured that GT40s were kept supplied with parts. Eventually, in the early 'eighties, an approach to the company was made by Safir Engineering Limited, headed by Peter Thorp. The proposal was for the manufacture of GT40s to be recommenced, with the approval of JW

Automotive Engineering Limited, and for the new cars, built in strictly limited numbers, to be called the GT40 Mark V. The deal was done, and the Mark V was born. It isn't a Ford – legal and liability reasons have prevented that – but the Mark V is a GT40, one of only two latter day types to be accorded that privilege.

The GT40 Mark V is very similar to an original Ford GT40, and externally is almost indistinguishable. Under the skin, the chassis shows distinct differences, these being penned by Len Bailey (one of the original design team which worked on the first Ford GTs) and intended to simplify what most agree to have been an over-engineered, over-complex tub. Chassis numbers range from GT40P/1090 to 1100, and from 1115 onwards.

The Holman GT-40 P Mark II

The latest (and probably last) car to be entitled to use the GT40 name is a Mark II built in Charlotte, North Carolina, by Lee Holman, a former GT40

team member. Holman & Moody Inc. were active during the mid-'sixties, campaigning Mark IIs as back-up to the Shelby American team. For many years they continued to provide maintenance for existing GT40s, until they eventually commenced the build of their own brand new Mark II, marketed by Holman Automotive Inc.

The Holman Mark II, available in both II-A and II-B specification, is based on a British-built chassis produced by Tennant Panels, who use a mixture of original tools and new ones made from original drawings. Completed tubs are shipped to the USA, where they are built into cars which are virtual clones of the Mark II of 1966 and 1967. The new Mark II features all necessary chassis, suspension and drive-train modifications which distinguished the Mark II from the GT40, and Holman Moody's status as a manufacturer of the original cars has ensured that the company has

the legal right to use the GT40 name. The company still has all the records necessary for it to duplicate the specification of any particular Mark II campaigned by the H&M team in 1966 and 1967, so a purchaser can buy a car which he knows is an exact duplicate of one raced during one of the classic endurance events of 1966 and 1967. Chassis numbers of the Holman Mark IIs start at GT40P 201.

76 Horsepower

Mention "76 horsepower" to any GT40 aficionado, and he'll know immediately what you mean. The words date back to 1967 when Ford's Roy Lunn presented a technical paper to the USA's Society of Automotive Engineers. In the paper Lunn mentioned that the prototype GT40's internal air ducting was absorbing precisely 76 of the 350 brake horsepower which the 255 cubic engine was producing, although Ford's designers had calculated the power losses would be no greater than 30 horsepower.

The reason for the surprisingly high power losses lay in the complexity of the ventilation systems designed for the new car. Despite being of a similar configuration to Lola's Mark 6 sports car, two examples of which Ford used as development hacks, the Ford GT was essentially a brand new car designed by a concern which had no previous experience in sports car building and racing. Consequently, every aspect of the car's design was approached from a fresh viewpoint, using Ford's state-of-the-art technology.

A classic example of Ford's then naiveté in design concerned the wind-tunnel tests conducted using a 3/8th scale model, in the tunnel of the University of Maryland. The target was low drag, which was achieved, but little or no thought was given to downforce, which turned out to be as low as the drag; as a result, the first cars built had commendably slippery shapes, but were dangerously unstable because of the lift generated by their too-smooth bodywork. To give Ford appropriate credit, their learning curve was extremely steep, and at the close of the GT project, in 1967, Ford had in their armoury the most advanced sports-racing car the world had ever seen.

The 76 horsepower disappeared in a variety of ways, from the front of the car to the back, but largely in the middle. The accompanying diagram shows just how cleverly the air in a GT40 was moved, but it is interesting to note how evolution did in fact change it in several ways.

The blue arrows show, at the front of the car, how air for cooling the engine entered below the rather high nose, went through the radiator, then exited through two grilles in the top of the nose panel. This arrangement was basically sound, but much too restrictive,

Above

When the driver's door was shut, the duct running through it lined up with this oval cut through the rear bulkhead. A similar feature was used on the passenger's side of the car. (Photo: Ford)

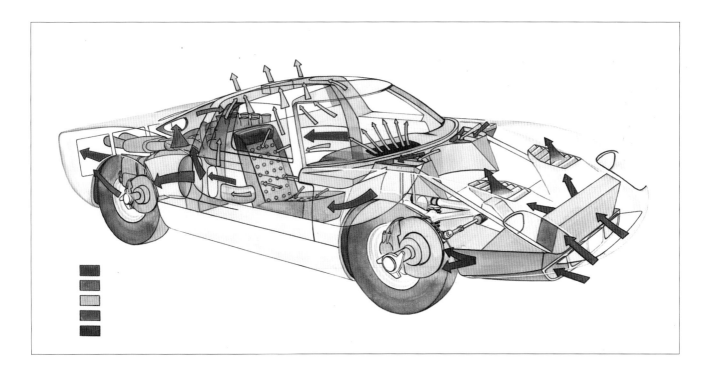

Above
*Where that 76 horsepower went – red for engine compart-
ment, brown for induction, yellow for the cockpit, green for
brakes, and blue for engine water and oil. (Ford Motor
Company)*

The nose had been unduly cluttered with equipment, and the placement of the peculiarly-shaped oil
tank, surrounding the spare wheel, had resulted in
the outlet passages being too small and convoluted.
Matters were not righted until the advent of the
definitive "Le Mans" nose, in June 1965, when for the
first time there appeared in the top of the nose two
large triangular air outlets which at last gave the
cooling air a direct and unrestricted exit from the
radiator. This new layout was made possible by the
repositioning of the spare wheel, and the replacing of
aluminium dry-sump engines with cast-iron wet-sump
versions, the latter not requiring a remote oil-tank.

Beneath the nose, an air-dam was fitted. Initially
the two central compartments of the air-dam held
long-range driving lamps, and the outer two slots fed
cooling air (arrowed green) direct to the front
brakes. The air-dam had been necessary to reduce
some of the front-end lift which the car's nose generated, but in this it was only partially successful. The
brake air ducts were perforce relocated when the Le
Mans nose arrived, but were still in basically the same
positions as before. However, by 1967, and the
arrival of the Mark IV and Mark II-B, it was realised
that directing ambient temperature air on to the

brakes could cause the discs to crack. So the front
brake air ducts had their intakes repositioned to
within a transverse panel immediately behind the
radiator. The air they passed to the brakes was
therefore warm, not cold, but of course it was still
significantly colder than the brakes upon which it was
directed.

At the base of the windscreen, a pair of bifurcated
inlets located in a high pressure area took in air for
cockpit cooling (yellow arrows) and for the engine
bay (red arrows). The cockpit air entered the driving
compartment through a grille located on top of the
dashboard. Production versions of the GT40 standardised on a grille taken from the British Ford
Zephyr/Zodiac range, and in recent years builders of
replica GT40s have ensured that by now no junkyard
Zephyr in the Western Hemisphere retains its demis-
ter grille.

Once in the cockpit, the air had to find its way

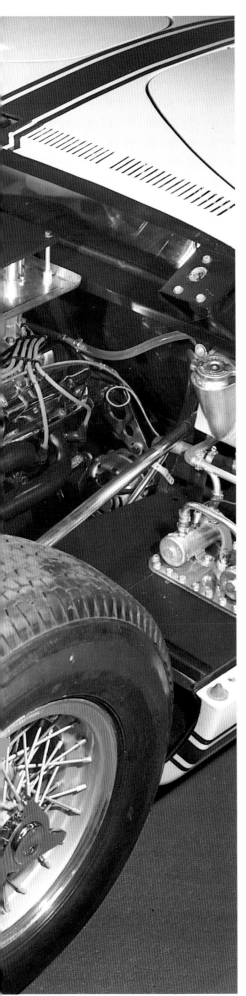

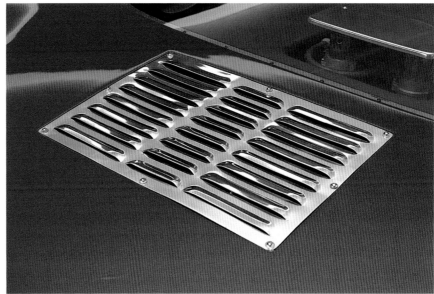

Above

This is the standardised version of the grille which was let in to the rear deck so as to allow hot air to escape from above the exhausts. (Photo: Gary Kohs)

Left

The prototype GT's engine bay shows on the left of the bulkhead the oval hole through which came the air to cool the fuel pumps and the engine bay generally. It was not long before the holes were blanked off. Note here the dark blue finish to the chassis, and the black exhausts. (Photo: Ford)

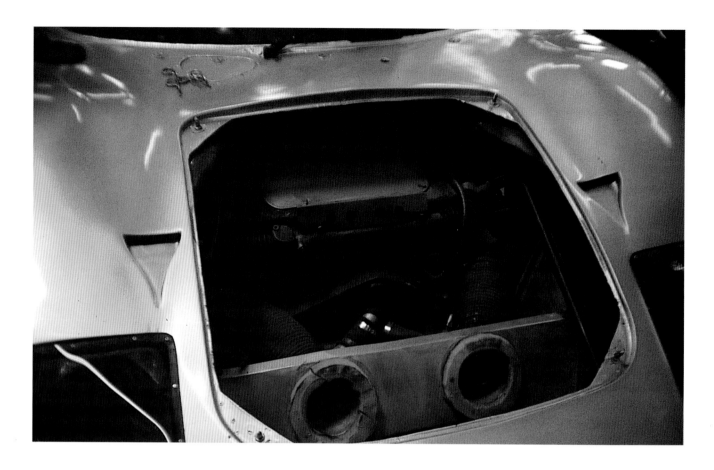

out, and to this problem Ford provided a novel solution. The seats' top surfaces were given a series of holes, which allowed the high-pressure air to enter the seats before being ducted into the box-section rear bulkhead, then exhausted through a row of small oblong holes cut into the top of the bulkhead. Note that, contrary to myth, the holes in the seats were designed to take air out of the cabin, not force it in. The two openings at the base of the screen were eventually replaced by a single NASA duct; two more NASA ducts, located further forward in the top of the front body panel, were added so as to provide air direct to the movable aeroflow "eyeballs" at each side of the dashboard.

The red arrows show the path of the air intended to cool the engine bay generally. Taking such air in at the front, when it was needed at the back, was ahead of its time. Its path took it through ducts moulded into the doors, through oval holes in both sides of the rear bulkhead, then over the fuel pumps, eventually to wash around the exhausts before leaving through two large grilles set into the back of the rear bodywork. It appears that a fair number of the 76 missing horses had bolted through these holes, and they were soon closed, never to be reopened. However, there is no doubt that the concept was basically sound, and it has subsequently been used on other racing cars, such as the Group C Lancia LC2 and the IMSA Ford Probe and Mustang GTP.

Initially, there was no provision for allowing the heat generated by the exhaust to find its way out

upwards, but before long a small grilled opening was provided immediately above the exhaust collector boxes; this was eventually enlarged substantially, and on the Mark II-A was provided with a transparent air-scoop which (in theory, at least) did not obstruct rearward vision. The engine breathed through two slender, sculptured, openings in the top of the rear bodywork, immediately behind the side windows (see brown arrows). This elegant and stylish solution proved perfectly adequate for all small-block GT40s, and was changed only when the 7-litre engine was installed in the Mark II variants.

Moulded into both sides of the rear bodywork were scoops which took air (green arrows) to the rear brakes. These too proved adequate, and (visually) were basically unchanged throughout Marks I to III, although their purpose was revised to provide air for oil coolers as well as brakes.

Above

Scoops for carburettor air were beautifully sculptured into the top of the rear bodywork. It could be argued that details such as this made the GT40 more than merely a racing car; it's a work of art. The lower air-scoops fed air to the rear brakes. Note that here a mesh grille is in place, a sure sign that the car in question is one built specifically for road use. (Photo: Gary Kohs).

During the period 1964 to 1967 Ford learned a great deal about the science (previously, art) of building a sports-racing car. The GT40s which in 1969 closed out the marque's racing career were still extremely close in overall design to the prototypes which in 1964 had stumbled so falteringly in their debut season – but their airflow systems had been honed so as not to lose nearly as much of that 76 horsepower.

On Track –
A Personal View

Ford keep two GT40s in their fleet, and both of them are entrusted to Bryan Wingfield, a long-time GT40 expert and aficionado who has forgotten more about what makes GT40s tick than most people will ever know. His duties involve keeping the two cars trackworthy and available for testing when required. With his co-operation, and Ford's readily given permission, courtesy of Don Hume, a date for a track test at Boreham was arranged. Both GT40s would be there for the day, just for my wife and me to play with. This was a dream come true.

Ford's GT40s have been in the ownership of the company from the time they were built. The newer of the pair is a silver-painted Mark III, chassis GT40M3/1107, the last Mark III to be built. It was used as a press demonstrator, and for a short time was taken to the USA, where Walter Hayes used it as a road car. The paintwork isn't original, but the car looks essentially the same now as it has always done.

Mark IIIs, as most readers will know, were built only as road cars, and none was ever raced. For that reason, there are a few people who think of the Mark III as being something of a poor relation, but in my view this attitude is unjustified. The chassis of the Mark III started out as being exactly the same as that of the Mark I racer, and the only real differences between racers and road cars are body styles (and remember, body panels can easily be changed), interior trim levels (including sound-deadening material) and central gearchange (which also can be easily changed), and suspension settings. The message (or at least my opinion) should by now be clear: a Mark III, built on a modified Mark I tub, is no more than a variant of a Mark I racer, and the former can be turned into the latter should its owner so wish.

Mark IIIs have a centrally-mounted gear change, which often comes in for criticism. The gear linkage is routed around the engine before it reaches the side of the ZF gearbox, and in the process it is said to lose much of its precision. 1107's gear change has come in for as much abuse as criticism, because most drivers, unused to the sequential nature of the change, insist on trying to skip gears, usually whilst the car is stationary. The most common scenario is that somebody brings the car to a standstill, in third gear, then puts the lever in neutral and switches off the engine. The next driver takes over and, not unreasonably, after starting the car tries to select first gear. However, the sequential change requires that because the car had stopped in third gear, second must be selected before first can be. What usually happens then is that the driver attempts to force the lever into the first gear position, and in so doing damages the locking mechanism, causing the change to balk.

Bryan Wingfield has removed the sequential locking mechanism, and in the process has made the Mark III's gearshift substantially easier to use than it was before.

Britain in October can be every bit as cold and wet as Britain at any other time of the year, but on this occasion the sun shone, quickly dispelling the early mist, and the temperature on an almost breeze-free day rose to levels sufficient to render multiple layers of coats unnecessary. It was a perfect day for a

Above

Open wide, and say aah... GT40s can look good even when opened up. The spare wheel cover is hinged, as on the Mark II racers. Door windows have a sideways opening panel which allows a little more ventilation than found in Mark Is, but it's hardly any more convenient for toll booths.

track-test. My introduction to the Mark III was with Bryan's assistant, Paul Fleming, at the wheel. We climbed into the car, in the process walking over the wide sills. This is almost inevitable, and any attempt to cross the sills without actually standing on them is unlikely to prove successful. It's usually better to stand on the seat, too, before sliding down into position. The lap and shoulder belts are generally not enough to stop passengers sliding ever lower into the seat, but the seats give ample side support.

The view out of the front is almost like looking down a wide valley, the raised fenders cutting off a lot of the view sideways.

We did a handful of laps with Paul driving. He pointed out what few features there are on the circuit, and explained some of the problems to be found on specific corners. There wasn't a great deal to watch for, except that on two right-hand corners the Armco was perilously close to the outside of the track; Armco being stronger than fibreglass, both

those corners required particular care. The first of the two had adverse camber, and the second had a double apex.

The experience for the passenger was as might be expected: strong acceleration, remarkable stopping power, and a degree of cornering substantially better than you'd expect from even a good road sports car. The "eyeball" vent was at first a nuisance, blowing too strongly in my face, but it was easily adjusted to direct air elsewhere. At least it was providing a good strong flow to cool the interior. Then it was my turn; at last, I could get behind the wheel of a GT40.

Track tests of GT40s are not new; they have been

Above and left

The Mark III's elongated tail is very different from that of the Mark I. The token bumpers give a little protection to the fibre-glass, and the exhaust is rerouted to below the engine, allowing the upper part of the bodywork to house a rudimentary luggage box.

undertaken since very early in the GT40's career, and became widespread as soon as Ford had a demonstrator or two in their fleet. This track test is, however, a little different from most of the others which have graced the pages of every motoring magazine with even the slightest sporting pretensions – it is written by somebody who does not spend his life

regularly sampling exotic high-performance cars provided free of charge by manufacturers looking for ever more column inches in a magazine.

Most track testers write from a perspective of considerable experience. Prior to being let loose with the GT40s, my only on-track experience consisted of a course of instruction at Bob Bondurant's driving school just outside Phoenix, Arizona. In four days of intense activity those excellent tutors at Bondurant's managed somehow to drill into me the rudiments of race-car driving, both in Mustang GTs (3 days) and Formula Fords (1 day). I learned of the fundamental handling differences between a front-engined car which understeered, and a mid-engined one which wanted to do just the opposite. Thus it was that, when faced with the Mark III, I felt at least that I wouldn't be embarrassingly slow or dangerous.

The driving seat was no different from the passenger's, but because of the wheel itself I didn't feel as if I would slide forward as much as had been the case when I had been a passenger. The wheel is smaller than standard, to permit more portly drivers to fit under it. The engine started on the first push of the button, and that delightful V8 rumble filled the cockpit. The clutch was surprisingly light (Ferrari please take note) and first gear was selected without a hitch. The pedals are different from the Mark I, and closer together. The clutch was fierce, and the revs had to be kept up to prevent stalling as we ambled out on to the track, the engine hunting as we did so. Thankfully, I didn't suffer the ignominy of stalling it. I drove the Mark III gently for a couple of laps, getting used to the feel of the clutch, gearchange and the throttle. I didn't attempt to double-declutch (the ZF gearbox has synchromesh, which renders it relatively unnecessary) and, as Paul had said that he didn't bother to heel-and-toe, neither did I.

The Bondurant experience proved invaluable, as I had a degree of confidence which I wouldn't otherwise have had, and after two slow laps I began to use more of the car's power and roadholding, and felt that I was at least quick, though hardly an expert.

Above

1107 displays its Mark III features of bumperettes, quad headlights, and parking lights which look suspiciously like those found on MG 1100s and a host of kit cars from the sixties.

Right

Mark IIIs had upholstery without the ventilation holes found on Mark Is. Gearchange was centrally mounted, and carpets covered the sills. The steering wheel on 1107 is smaller than standard, to allow the car to be used by children.

A few more laps, and Paul was then satisfied (or scared) enough to vacate the passenger seat, and let my wife join me in the car.

It was surprising to find that there was little tyre noise, and I had expected to hear the tyres protesting somewhat, but there was in fact more noise from the clutch, which yelped on every upchange. Paul said that the only time it wouldn't squeal would be on a very quick change from fourth to fifth, and this did prove to be the case. 1107's suspension is harder than the average Mark III, but still softer than found on pukka race cars. The track surface at Boreham is quite poor, with pebbles strewn across it where the rally Escort Cosworths had come on to it from the

gravel areas. The surface was generally bad, with the concrete ribbed and broken in places. The Mark III's suspension seemed to pick up and magnify every bump, and the harsh ride and noisy engine meant that the GT40 was rather tiring to drive.

The engine felt to have lots of power. It was a solid-lifter 302 (serial "302/01", although Bryan said he suspected it was actually a 289), producing somewhere around 300bhp on the 1969 scale, which in 1990's terms might mean about 270 SAE net. With only a ton to propel, it felt spectacularly powerful, and the torque was such that it seemed to matter little which gear was selected. Long throttle travel meant that it would not be easy for the lead-footed

Left

The profile of the GT40 is one of the most beautiful views of the car – but then, all views are good, aren't they? Note that five-spoke wheels, Alan Mann-style, have replaced the original Borrani wires. The name on the door is in honour of the car being driven recently by a certain Italian-American racer; the author is not expecting his own name to replace Andretti's.

right hand corner, on the outside of which was the temporary "pits" housing the other GT40, plus a handful of road cars, the trailer etc. Thus it was important not to get that corner wrong, as an "off" would be expensive. It was there that I discovered that the brakes weren't in as good condition as they might have been. Going into the corner a little faster than previously, and braking fairly hard, the Mark III began to shimmy badly, and I half expected to perform a gyration in front of the handful of spectators; my heart missed a beat or two before I got it all back together again, and continued, a little chastened.

Not long after, at a different corner, the same thing happened again, so from that point on I was very wary of the brakes. They were extremely, reassuringly, powerful, but couldn't be relied on in the extreme. Bryan explained later that one of the discs was warped, and would shortly be removed and reskimmed. That did at least restore some of my faith in me, if not in the brakes.

On one other occasion I went a little too fast into a left hand bend, and felt the tail beginning to slide out. A touch of correction on the steering wheel and the slide was corrected easily and undramatically. I got the impression that the Mark III was a forgiving car which would be unlikely to bite the unwary. The only other thing to give me cause for concern was when I noticed that the front body insert, covering the spare wheel, began to lift in proportion to speed. Expecting to lose it at any moment, a quick pit stop was called for. There I was reassured that it always lifts, so it was back to the track for more.

At the stop Bryan commented that every time we passed, he could see my wife grinning from ear to

to get it wrong dramatically; you really have to push that pedal a long way down before the full-throttle stop. On the longest straight the speedometer, with needle wobbling in time with the bumps in the road, suggested that we were doing 155mph; Bryan explained later that the speedometer exaggerated by 17%, and our true speed was probably around 133mph. However, the rough track meant that it was quite fast enough for me, and my top speed was limited more by apprehension about keeping the front wheels on the ground than by the engine's power-curve. I take my hat off to the stalwarts who actually raced these things at the Targa Florio.

At the end of the longest straight is a sweeping

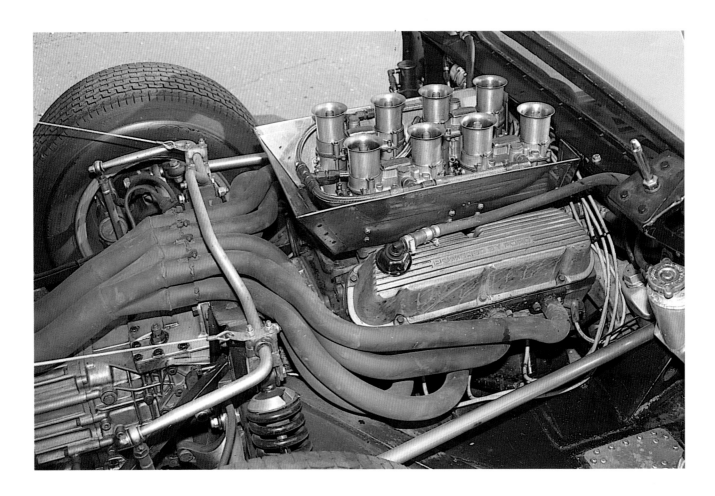

Above

1008's engine bay reveals the lack of a crossover exhaust system.

ear as she enjoyed the trip. Clearly she was unaware of my limitations as a race car driver. A little later, as experience built up and I began to lap more quickly, the combination of warm sun streaming in through the big windscreen, the very comfortable reclining seat and the substantial engine noise conspired to let her drift into sleep!

A short time later the car ground to a halt out on the circuit, the fuel pumps whirring frantically as they sought more petrol. The switch on the passenger side was thrown to allow the car to pick up from the other tank, and we got underway again.

The view out of the back of GT40s has often been criticised. The rear window is almost flat, so the large area translates into a very narrow horizontal slit. However, I had no trouble at all spotting and identifying one of the works rally-car testers in an Escort Cosworth closing rapidly; that was in broad daylight, but whether it would be so easy to identify a police patrol car at night is a different matter.

I thoroughly enjoyed my time in the Mark III. In my opinion it was easy to handle, had a delightful gearchange, masses of power, and more than enough cornering ability to satisfy me. It was comfortable and, (by comparison with the Mark I) not particularly noisy.

It was hot, and on a really warm day would probably be unpleasantly so. Its low height caused no difficulties on the track, but my experience of several years' ownership of a Marcos, with a height of 43 inches, suggests that on the road its forward visibility would become more of a problem. I really liked the Mark III. Would I enjoy owning and running one? Absolutely, but as a fun car only. When it comes to the usual cut-and-thrust of driving on Britain's appallingly congested roads, I'd stick with another

Ford V8 – my air-conditioned, automatic-transmission Mustang is much better for everyday use. perhaps it would be a different story on the open roads of mid-west America...

The older of Ford's two GT40s is GT40P/1008, built in 1965 and used extensively that year and in early 1966 as a press demonstrator.

It has featured in many a magazine article, and will no doubt continue to do so for a long time to come. When new it was given an outing by John Blunsden, who drove it for Motor Racing magazine, and in the process succeeded in breaking Brands Hatch's lap record for GT cars. In late 1966 it was rebodied as a Mark II, and began many years of service as a show car, pretending to be the 1966 Le Mans winner. It was later rebodied again, as a lookalike of the 1968/69 Le Mans winner, and continued to do duty at displays throughout Britain.

Eventually 1008 wound up in Ford's collection at Swansea, where it languished unloved for some time

before Bryan persuaded Ford to allow him to take custody of the car and turn it once more into an actual runner – in the process fitting an engine in the car, and replacing the dummy equipment with parts that actually worked. 1008 is now back in the Linden Green which it wore when new, although on modern film it tends to look a little less brown than it does in pictures taken back in 1965.

1008's clutch was fiercer than 1107's. It was coupled to the same type of ZF Gearbox, (although with the synchromesh rather well-worn) with a right-hand shift lever, but the gear change itself retains the sequential locks which don't allow for missing a shift. It's a good idea, for it prevents the driver missing a

47

shift and accidentally over-revving the engine. My initial opinion of the gear change was unfavourable. When attempting to change down for a corner I found myself changing up instead. The reason was obvious: I was not giving enough sideways pressure on the shift lever. It was also easy to correct. Bearing in mind that, for example, it is impossible to shift from fifth to second, all you have to do is to ensure that you apply sideways pressure in the direction you want the lever to go; the lockouts make certain that you won't miss a gear. Once I had stopped worrying about the price of ZF gearboxes and Ford perhaps being disgruntled if I blew an engine, the gear change became a delight.

1008's engine was a low-specification 289 which had been rescued from a junkyard. It had been chosen because 1008's ZF already had a bellhousing

welded to it, so an early engine was needed to mate with the existing bellhousing. The 289's power output has not been measured, but it must be substantially less that the solid lifter 302's in 1107. The chances are that in a 1960's car it was originally rated at around 220bhp; with the addition of a free-flow exhaust system (non-crossover) it will have gained some power, and the four Webers will have added around forty more. However, horsepower ratings quoted in the '60s were optimistic in the extreme, so the probability is that the engine now provides somewhere around the 220 horses it was supposed to have in the first place.

The choice of a non-crossover exhaust system may appear puzzling, but there is a sound practical reason for it. Either side's system can be removed quickly, without affecting the opposite side. One

and Paul said that he liked to heel-and-toe, but within the timetable available I elected not to practice such procedures, and relied on the synchromesh plus the fact that the car was slower than the Mark III.

The lack of power was very noticeable in a straight line, the car feeling distinctly slower. All things are relative, and compared with most road cars the GT40 was still very quick, as a 220bhp/ton car should be. The Mark III's 300bhp/ton was so much better, nevertheless. However, it was rather misleading to look at the speedometer and find that the car was travelling substantially more slowly than the Mark III had done. 1008's ZF has an adjuster which allows for the speedometer to be adjusted to show the correct speed, for tachograph purposes, so Bryan had set the speedo accurately, thus making it read 17% less than on 1107.

At the start of the day, 1008 had an obvious engine misfire, but this had gone by the time I began my stint in it. Later, the misfire returned, and I was happy to swap 1008 for 1107. My confidence was greater in 1107, due in part to 1107 having passenger-side seatbelts, which 1008 did not. In the event of my making a mess of things, I had no wish to have to peel my passenger from the windscreen.

My overall view of the Mark I is that it needed more power (as if I could use it!) and that it was too noisy by half, but then that could easily be cured, by earplugs if nothing else. Its visibility definitely needed improvement, there being no side mirrors fitted – but real racing drivers wouldn't use them anyway. Basically, for use as a race car it would be great, but for road use it needed civilising – which is exactly what has happened to 1107. When my lottery numbers come up, I won't need counselling as to how to cope with the sudden wealth – there are still six other Mark IIIs out there, one will be for sale...

interesting outcome of the two systems not having any connection is that the engine sounds different, having the distinctive beat associated with Cobras and many V8-powered road cars.

On the track, the Mark I felt quite different from the Mark III, although one point of similarity was that the nose insert had a tendency to lift as speed increased. The car felt harder and sounded much noisier, the latter due to its lack of carpets and sound-deadening material, and its open, unsilenced exhausts. The tyres were nearly new, pure racing specification, and not fully scrubbed-in (at least, not until later in the day). They would definitely provide the Mark I with more grip than the Mark III had, but the relative lack of power meant that the extra grip was wasted when accelerating out of corners.

The pedals were wider apart than on the Mark III,

Classic Class Reunions

Above

The 1990 edition of the Christie's Historic Festival at Silverstone brought together the UK's largest-ever gathering of GT40s, featuring all marks from I to V, including the Le Mans double-winner 1075. Visible here are 1000BW, 1002, 1003, 1006, 1007, 1008, 1012, 1013, 1025, 1047, 1053, 1065, 1066, 1075, 1084, 1107, J12, two Mark Vs, and 1127, a car recently built on a Tennant Panels chassis.

Left

It is likely that the 1990 Silverstone gathering could claim that never before had so many GT40s been gathered together under one (canvas) roof. Packing them in was not easy, but gave the author the opportunity to drive every one of them – or rather, to sit there and steer them, whilst everyone else pushed.

Above

Peter Teichmann's 1001 is now back in its Essex Wire colours, which suit it well. Note on the top of the car the four rows of vents which readily identify this car as one of the early series; between the middle two rows is the square hole in which resides the rear-bonnet catch.

Right

Ford France used 1003 a great deal in 1965 and 1966. It was later converted for road use, and after a time when it was allowed to become rather dishevelled it was acquired by Robert Horne, and restored to its former glory. (Photo: Robert Horne)

Opposite

Thanks to its registration number, 1002 will always be known as Felix. This much-raced early car lost its roof vents in a rebuild many years ago; its Mark III spare-wheel cover is a legacy of the period when it ran with a complete Mark III nose section, its first Le Mans nose having been all but destroyed in a road accident. Very few GT40 parts get thrown away, and much of 1002's damaged nose found itself fitted to 1112.

Above

One of the particularly happy aspects of historic race meetings is the opportunity for drivers to be reunited with their cars of yore. Here Sir John Whitmore poses with 1006, which he drove at Le Mans in 1965. 1006 was the first GT40 to wear the definitive "Le Mans" nose, and it is good to see the car now restored to its 1965 configuration.

Opposite

1007 and 1008, together in Bryan Wingfield's truck, provide a perfect example of how ad hoc modifications and repairs can change the shape of a car; the various air intakes on 1007 have ended up subtly but noticeably different from those on the standard 1008.

Above

It is appropriate that long-time Ford France stalwart 1007 should be French-owned. Here it is in 1986 at Le Mans, where it took part in the historic display. Its raised front fenders are thanks to it having received ex-Paul Hawkins bodywork. (Photo: Dave Cundy)

Below

Richard Morrison's 1010, seen here at Road America, is another GT40 to receive Essex Wire team colours, and it is now in concours condition. Interestingly, this is the second 1010, which never actually wore those Essex Wire colours in its racing days. The original 1010 was written off in a testing accident in 1966, and its chassis was destroyed. Later, some of its parts were used in building a car around a new officially-supplied chassis, which was given the same number as its predecessor. In 1969 the new 1010 was raced extensively by Peter Sadler, and it gave a good account of itself in various major races, including Le Mans.

Below left

On the roof of 1012 can be seen the rectangular block of air vents which are typical of Mark IIs. Note also that, again typical of Mark IIs, there is no NASA duct at the base of the windshield.

Above

1012 is one of many GT40s to have had a chequered history. Written-off in a testing accident at Daytona, the remains of the chassis were delivered to a junkyard, from where they were later rescued. They passed through various hands until they found their way to England, where a rebuild commenced. At first the intention was that all existing parts of the chassis would be retained and straightened, but the enormity of the task led to work being halted, then recommenced with the most badly damaged sections replaced with new parts from Tennant Panels. Bryan Wingfield oversaw the rebuild, and when 1012 eventually re-emerged it was in perfect condition. The restoration included the remanufacture, at enormous cost, of a single example of the Ford/Kar Kraft T-44 gearbox.

Above left

With 1013 safely loaded upon its trailer, the late Steven Smith lights a cigar prior to commencing the journey from Silverstone back to the frozen North of England. 1013 was the first GT40 to be produced in road car trim, but by 1991, when this picture was taken, there was little on 1013 to give the game away. Between 1966 and 1991, 1013 had seen a great deal of use, as an all-weather commuter and vintage racer. At the time of writing 1013 is with Bryan Wingfield for restoration to road car standards.

Above

Early GT40s featured separate rear lights and indicator lights on each side of the rear body panel, as seen here on 1014 at Road America. At the 1966 Mont Ventoux hill-climb, 1014 finished second, beaten only by Ford France's 1003.

Left

Having spent many years in an all-white colour scheme, Shelby team car 1015 has at last been restored to the condition it was in when it almost won Le Mans. The dayglo red identity panels on the front body had been added after a pits incident, in which a Le Mans Ford team mechanic was nearly run over by 1017, which was also painted pale blue. At Road America, Brian Mimaki drove this beautiful Mark II-A to a tenth place finish in the GT40s race, at an average speed of 88.607mph.

Above and left

Third place at Le Mans in 1966 went to Holman & Moody's 1016, which for several years was painted to represent 1015. Holman & Moody had been in charge of 1016 at Le Mans, and after the race they received a letter from Ford's Don Frey, thanking them for the part they had played in the Le Mans victory, specifically expressing thanks for the fact that H&M accepted their role as back-up to the Shelby American team. This serves to explain why Holman & Moody's results were never as good as Shelby's. At Road America, DK Associates' Mark II-A was driven by Ken Quintenz, but it didn't take part in the GT40s race.

Above

In the late sixties 1021 was best known for being the maroon GT40 with the grotesque bulge on its roof. Now it's much prettier, and in Brian Redman's hands it's quite fast too. Low down on the front fenders can be seen the canard fins which were fitted to the car on the Friday of the Road America weekend; these give additional downforce.

Above right

When Chris Hutchings' 1017 arrived at Road America it was in concours condition, thanks to a recent total restoration by Massachusetts-based Paul Russell and Company. The result was the prize for Best Mark I GT40 at the reunion. 1017 has been restored to its Le Mans 1966 trim, complete with identification lamp mounted in the rear fender.

Right

1018 has spent much of its life in Australia, but is now back in the USA, with California-based Saguro Kato. Although 1018 carries Gulf racing colours, it was originally delivered as a show car, and was never intended for racing. It is seen here in Road America's pit-lane, in company with 1057 and XGT-3.

Right

Lime Rock Park, Connecticut, is the location for this picture of 1019, driven by New Jersey-based Paul Reisman in the 1991 BMW Vintage Festival. The car shows several features of interest, including the ribs pressed into the chassis sides, which are unusual in not being covered by fibreglass appliqué panels. The doors and front body panel have been turned in slightly so as to meet the top of the chassis, this being a feature of this car and also of AM.GT40.2, the other ex-Paul Hawkins racer; note also the Mark IV-style sliding panel in the side window.

Above

In June 1991, when the Musée Automobile de la Sarthe moved into its superb new Le Mans premises, GT40P/1020/67 was a star attraction. It is seen here before the official opening. 1020 was chosen to star in the museum's official poster, on which was a beautiful painting of the GT40 leaping out from a gilded picture frame. Unfortunately, this old Ford France car, which raced at Le Mans in 1967, is still in rather a dilapidated condition, with ill-fitting body panels, and sub-standard paintwork; it is crying out for restoration. Please don't let that put anyone off visiting the museum, which is both interesting and imaginative in the way it displays its 85 cars. (Photo: Musée Automobile de la Sarthe)

Above right

At the time of writing, Croft Autodrome in Northern England was about to reopen as a venue for historic racing. 1022 is shown there back in 1973 at a FordSport day, shortly before it began raining again.

Right

Richard Cohen's 1023 has been restored to the colour scheme it wore back in 1967, when it was raced by John Harris, driving for Malcolm Gartian; it was eventually replace by a Lola T-70 Mark III GT. 1023 lost this colour scheme way back in 1969. Parked behind the GT40 is Greg Mathew's 1965 McLaren Mk3B.

Overleaf

Richard Cohen drove 1023 to 11th position in the GT40s race at Road America; his average speed was 86.436mph. Here the GT40 is seen heading towards Turn 3.

Above

David Cohen, in 1024, is held at Road America's assembly area as 1076 is waved through. Have there ever been any other GT40s on Hoosier tyres? 1024, which is now US-resident, finished the GT40s race in sixth position, with an average speed of 93.419mph.

Above right

1024's major claim to fame is that it was once a school car at the Bob Bondurant School of High Performance Driving, at Sears Point, California. Its main purpose there was to give demonstrations to visitors, rather than to allow hot-shoe hopefuls to practice in it.

Right

1025 is another unusually-shod GT40, wearing Avon rubber when seen here rounding Copse at the Silverstone Historic meeting in 1991.

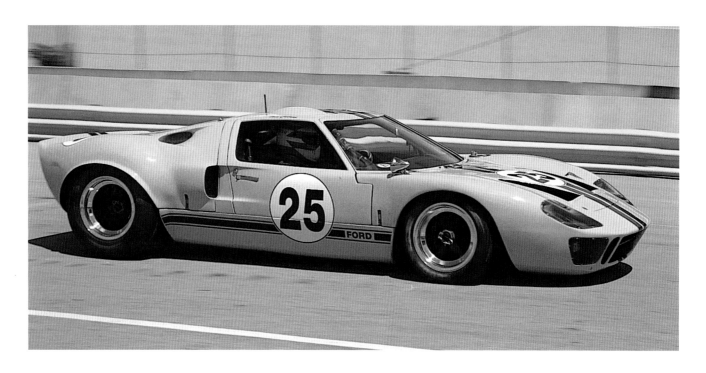

Above and right

By 1994, 1025 had moved to the USA, changed its coat, put on more usual boots, and was owned by Tom Celani. It is interesting to see that it still has the roof bulge, and the flared rear fenders and chassis appliqué panels. In these views radio-equipped 1025 is seen on Road America's pit entry road, and in the pit-lane itself.

Left

When the Good Year Eagles are removed, 1025's engine bay reveals radially-ventilated discs and the rear suspension. The burnished exhaust pipes are a full crossover system, but rarely when GT40s were raced did the pipes look as beautiful as these.

Above left

Jeff Lewis brought 1026 all the way from California to attend the Road America reunion, and then he ended up having to push the car himself; the author could have helped, but then cameras do tend to get in the way, and it would have been a pity to have them damage the paintwork. 1026 is in Essex Wire livery, and carries the number it wore when it won the Sports category in the 1966 Sebring 12-hour race, and came third overall.

Left

1026 is as clean under the skin as it is above it. This view of the underbonnet area shows the semi-circular bay originally intended to house the spare wheel, when such things were narrower than they eventually became. It is strange that, despite the spare wheel being moved forward, the cut-out remained in the GT40 chassis right to the very end of production.

Above

1027 is back in the colours it wore when it was on display at the 1966 Brussels salon. The car spent many of its years in Jim Toensing's ownership, and in residence at the Briggs Cunningham collection, but with the sale of the collection to the Colliers, 1027 had to find a new home. For several years it has been owned by James Ladwig.

Above

For many years 1032, then thought to be the 1966 Le Mans winner, was an exhibit in first the Indy Hall of Fame, and then the Museum of Early Wheels at Terre Haute, Indiana. It has since been transferred back to the Indianapolis Motor Speedway, and is again on display at their superb Hall of Fame, which contains several sports cars as well as the more obvious Indy cars. Apart from its spurious colour scheme it is in delightfully original condition, a perfect example of what a Mark II-A should be.

Right

1031 is one of several GT40s to have suffered an identity crisis. Available evidence suggests that this is the car which is currently resident in France, but which carries the serial number 1047; it appears that the switch was made to smooth customs formalities when the car was sent to France to take part in a series of races at the end of the 1967 season. This detail-packed historical picture shows 1031 in its heyday, being prepared for the 1966 Le Mans 24 hours, where it was driven by Mario Andretti and Lucien Bianchi. Preparation took place in a partitioned-off part of a local Peugeot garage, and only a few yards away from 1031 French mechanics were busy giving routine services to family saloons. (Photo: Ford)

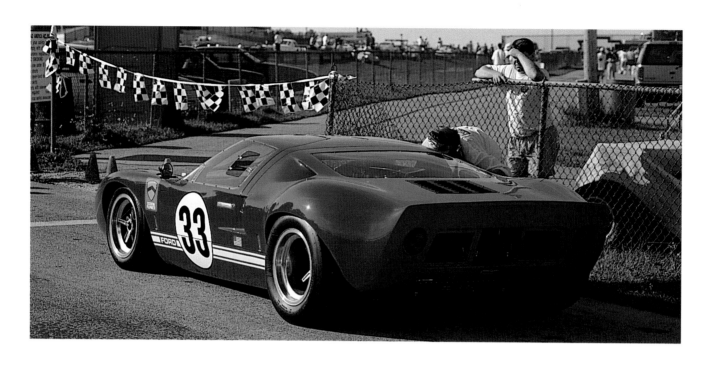

Above

1035 spent much of its life in England, where at one time it was a member of the Shell parachute-equipped team. Eventually it emigrated to Japan, from where owner Yoshitami Hirabayashi brought it all the way to Road America. The car still carries a 1968-vintage FordSport club badge in its radiator opening.

Above left and left

Georges Filipinetti's unloved road car, 1033, was sold by the Swiss Scuderia owner and became a racer. Its racing career over and once more a road car, it was almost destroyed in a roadside fire. It is now in excellent condition, and at Road America was driven by its owner, Tom Armstrong. An average speed of 95.844mph gave it fourth place in the GT40s race.

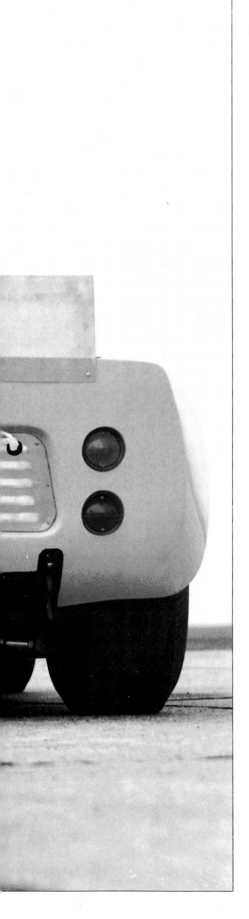

Above

*Robert Ash, proprietor of the FAV Company, of Norcross, Georgia, made an excellent
job of restoring James Jaeger's 1036 to the condition seen here at Road America.
1036 was also a member of Shell's group of parachute-equipped GT40s, but it is now
unique as the only one of the four to carry, once again, a braking 'chute.*

Left

*A (small) apology is called for here. This picture is, obviously, not in colour. However,
its historical interest more than justifies its inclusion in an otherwise all-colour book.
The year was 1967 (look at the fashion styles) and the car is 1035, fitted with its
braking parachute, mounted centrally on the top of the rear bodywork. 1035 was one
of four light blue GT40s which took part in the Shell advertising campaign which featured parachute-assisted stops. (Photo: Ford)*

Above

The GT40's low height is all the more apparent when it is seen alongside a Corvette, hardly the John Wayne of the automotive world itself.

Right

1040 has been one of those GT40s which have seen more than their fair share of low moments. This one occurred in 1966, at Le Mans. Filipinetti's 1040 had outlasted all the other GT40s, and was looking set for a fifth place overall, and first in class, when it skidded on the approach to the Esses, apparently on fuel thrown out of its filler caps under braking; driver Dieter Spoerry then became a passenger as 1040 headed for the earth banking. The Le Mans plombeurs have much to answer for. Subsequent examination of 1040's engine found it to be in good condition, and the car could have been expected to complete the race distance. Note in this view the skid marks, the piece of 1040's tail dumped onto its nose, and the rear wheel and drive shaft sitting nearby. Safety standards were different in those days, but in the 1990s an obstruction such as this would NOT be left on the track to be a hazard for everyone else. (Photo: Ford)

Right

With its road car heritage well-hidden, the Mimakis' 1043 looks very much the race car, thanks to its fully-ducted spare wheel cover. Halibrand wheels, hardly visible here, add to the race car look.

Below

1045 is probably best known as the Girling car, although it remained with that company for only two years. In the Hamilton family's ownership the car became metallic light green, and was featured in several magazine articles, including a full-colour track test in the French magazine Retro Viseur, as late as August 1990. Although 1045 is US-based, it is owned by Briton John Constable.

Below right

At Dearborn in 1986, George Stauffer showed 1046, part way through its restoration. It gave a good opportunity to see what a Mark II really looks like under the skin.

1046 only raced twice — at Le Mans 1966, where it won, and at Daytona in 1967, where it retired with transmission problems. Now it is fully restored to its 1966 Mark II-A configuration, but retains its 1967 Holman & Moody rollcage.

Above

Jim Kinsler actually uses road car 1050 on the road, an otherwise rare occurrence for a GT40 nowadays, driving it to his workplace in Detroit on days when rain is definitely not even a long shot in the forecast.

Below

The photo session at Road America took far longer than anyone had envisaged, due to the problem of arranging the forty-plus cars so that they would all appear at once in a single panoramic picture. Here Fran Kress's road car 1054, wearing the author's favourite GT40 livery, is manhandled into position.

Right

1051, a former road car wearing full ex-works Gulf bodywork, lines up ahead of 1025 and 1083 in Road America's assembly area. Chris MacAllister finished fifth in the GT40s race.

Below

Chris MacAllister gets ready to take 1051 to the grid for the Enduro race at Road America. Chris's car was the only original GT40 taking part in the 26-lap Enduro, and out of 64 starters he finished a creditable seventh, only two laps behind the leaders. His average speed for the 70-minute race was 95.809mph.

Above

The year is 1982, and this is road car 1053 hiding in a corner of one of John Etheridge's outbuildings, awaiting a service. Since then, the car has been repainted, has lost its black stripes, and acquired the registration plate GTK 40.

Opposite

New Yorker Harvey Siegel vintage races 1058, which has had its Borranis replaced by magnesium Halibrands, firmer and more reliable than the original wire wheels, and capable of coping with stickier rubber. Prior to a practice session, Harvey's engineer stands by the open door to keep the Wisconsin sun off the race-suited driver within.

Left

Road car 1061 as it was in 1973, at the Croft FordSport day. The paintwork is unusual, as are the Mark II-style air scoops for the air-conditioning system.

Right

1062 is another road car enjoying a new lease of life in vintage racing, this time in Europe. Seen here at the Nürburgring, the car wears Halibrand wheels, and is driven by German Hans J Weber. (Photo: Jürgen Strehle)

Left

Jack Frost, owner of 1059 for over twenty years, brought his car to Road America for the Anniversary gathering. The car's white paintwork has a delightful pearlescent sheen, but its original tyres, long past their prime, prevent the car from doing any serious running.

Below

Greg Whitten's road car 1057, here in Road America's pit lane, is another GT40 beautifully restored by Robert Ash.

Above and left

Gary Kohs's 1063 is as near perfect an example of a GT40 road car as any can be; apart from the replacement of the Ford ovals on the sills by stripes, 1063 is in stock road car trim. Note the letters on the front of the nose, the door locks, and the grilles in the air intakes. (Photo: Gary Kohs)

Above left

1061 has been developed into one of the fastest of the present-day vintage-racing GT40s, brought up to full Gulf specification. This wide-tyred racer, owned by Arizona-based Jim Click, was driven by Don Roberts to second place in the Road America GT40s race, just 10.175 seconds behind Brian Redman.

Above

The registration plate "GT 40", formerly on 1010, adorned 1065 until eventually it was sold for a reputedly substantial sum, and was seen sometime later on the nose of a spaceframe GT40 lookalike. There is little on this car, seen here at Silverstone, to suggest that it was built to road specifications.

Left

Gulf-liveried 1066 is a road car in the T C Harrison collection, in Sheffield, and is seen here at Silverstone in 1990. When Ronnie Spain and the author visited the collection, John Harrison was unable to offer either of them a ride in 1066, so both had to make do with a consolation prize of a trip around the local streets in one of the Harrisons' Ferrari 250 GTOs!

Left

This is the second 1073, photographed at Croft FordSport day in 1971, and at that time owned by Glynis Childs. The original wearer of this number was written off at Brands Hatch in 1968, although its wrecked tub still exists. 1073 wore a widened rear body section (ex Paul Hawkins), and the four tail lights give it away as being originally one from an early car; the unusual five-spoke wheels are worthy of note.

Above Left

The 1972 Brands Hatch FordSport Day brought out GT40s aplenty. Ford's Mark III, 1107, follows Robert Danny's road car 1069. The chassis applique panels are missing from 1069, and 1107's number plate is positioned a little further back on the nose than it is today. (Photo: Dave Cundy)

Above

Gulf car 1074 was a member of the JW Automotive Engineering team in both 1968 and 1969, winning the 1968 Monza 1000km, and coming close to winning the same year's Watkins Glen 6-hours. Its regular drivers throughout 1968 were Paul Hawkins and David Hobbs. 1074 was turned into a roadster for filming Solar Productions' Le Mans, and when eventually rebuilt it ended up with a Mark III spare-wheel cover, and the wrong stripes on the nose. Now part of the Blackhawk Collection, at Road America 1074 was tended by Rick Cole; at Saturday night's charity auction Rick showed just how well a professional auctioneer does his job.

Above

1074's chassis is almost unique amongst GT40s, sharing with only 1075 the Mirage-style squared off section which on all other GT40s is semi-circular. The reason for this is that 1074 was once itself a Mirage, M/10003, and was rebuilt to GT40 configuration over the winter of 1967/68.

Left

For most people 1075 will always be the most famous of them all. With two victories at Le Mans, plus wins at Sebring, Watkins Glen, Brands Hatch and Spa, no other GT40 can come close to 1075's record.

Left

The business end of 1075. This is the view which most of its competitors saw of it in 1968 and 1969. Seen here at Silverstone, 1075 was in Peter Livanos's ownership; by the time it reached Road America it had been bought by Sam Walton, who entrusted the driving to Bill Kontes. In the GT40s race Bill finished ninth, covering ten laps at an average speed of 88.677mph.

Above left

The third regular member of the Gulf trio was 1076, seen here at Road America in company with 1075. Owned by the Zeigler Coach Co, Bruce Zeigler drove it to seventh place in the GT40s race. In its heyday, 1076 had led the 1969 Daytona 24-hours, with Ickx and Oliver sharing the driving, but a cracked cylinder block caused the car to begin to overheat, and it was to crash soon afterwards. Its highest place finish was a third at Le Mans in 1969.

Above

Like several other GT40s, 1078 is on its second chassis, the first having been destroyed in 1970. In its second incarnation 1078 came too late to be raced in earnest (it was finished only in 1978). It is seen here at Silverstone in 1991.

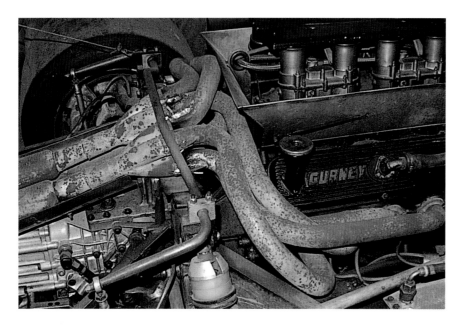

Above left

This is what a GT40's engine bay should not look like – but 1082's excuse is that it has been a rally car! Photographed when it was part of the Serge Pozzoli collection, near Paris, the ex-Michel Martin Ford France GT40 was on modular wheels, and looked well-used. It has since taken up residence in Switzerland.

Left

This is more like how we expect to see a GT40's engine bay. Like all GT40s from 1074 onwards, Jim George's 1083 has a Gurney-Weslake engine installed, but this one is unusual in being dry-sumped.

Above

Few GT40s have raced where 1080 has done. Sold at first to A. F. Pires in Angola, 1081 then went to Emilio Marta, who campaigned it enthusiastically in various African events. At one stage in its career it wore Gulf livery, and was fitted with makeshift fins. Eventually, Marta brought it to Portugal, but recently the car has found a new home in Switzerland. (Photo: Emilio Marta)

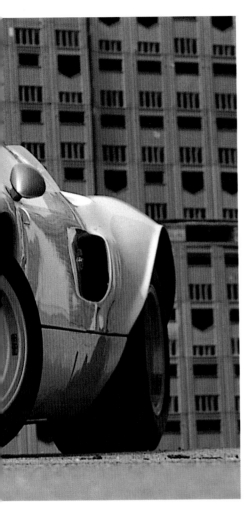

Left

The IGFA Deutsche Auto Zeitung GT40 was a new car for a new team in 1969. It took part in most of the major races that year, with several class wins, plus a splendid sixth place at Le Mans. It was then sold in Germany, for road use, before passing to its current owner Henri Bercher, who has recently completed a long and extremely thorough restoration. Henri at first painted 1081 in plain white, but at last he has added the three stripes which recall the car's racing days. Since completion of the restoration, 1081 has had a couple of visits to Le Mans, and is likely to take part in the historic reunions there for some time to come. (Photo: Georges Filliez)

Below

The author will not quickly forget being chauffeured around Silverstone in 1084, driven by Ray Mallock. Despite its high chassis number, the car is an old-timer, being a rebuild of 1965 Le Mans racer GT40P/1004. Although 1084 is a comparative heavyweight, it was used by JW Automotive Engineering at Spa in 1968, where it finished fourth (Ickx and Redman won, in 1075). Now in the ownership of Bell & Colvill, 1084 has been one of the most actively-campaigned GT40s in vintage racing. It is seen here with 1075 and "1047", at Silverstone in 1990.

Below left

1083 is reputed to have been raced by its first owner, the Colegio Arte e Instruccao, in local events in Brazil, before being sold to Wilson Fittipaldi. Here at Road America it is keeping company with 1025 and 1051.

Above left

The unfinished 1085 was despatched from Slough in March 1969 – and to this day has apparently not been completed. The gap in the chassis-number listing has been plugged by a new "1085A" (the number used with permission of the owner of the original car) built around a Sbarro chassis. The car had been assembled by Swiss Franco Sbarro, but was delivered to Bryan Wingfield, who modified it for competition use by its owner, René Herzog. Sbarro's chassis have thicker metal than the original ones did, and the body panels too are much thicker and heavier; this does, however, allow them to be an appreciably better fit than the pukka body sections.

Left

The last officially numbered Mark I GT40 was 1086, seen here at Watkins Glen in 1989. It was built on the last Abbey Panels chassis retained by JW Automotive Engineering, and was only completed in 1984. John Willment recently announced that three more official GT40s are to be assembled by his company; all three are expected to use Tennant Panels chassis, and will probably be assembled by Bryan Wingfield. They will carry chassis numbers 1087 to 1089.

Above

Rarely since the days of the factory production line have three Mark IIIs been seen together. These are 1102 (blue), 1104 (red) and 1106 (white), at Road America. (Sorry that didn't come out as red, white and blue, but we can't think of everything.) The lower rear corner of the side window on 1102 is curved; on both the other cars it is pointed, as found on all Mark IIIs from 1103 to 1107.

Right

At first glance 1106 looks just like an Essex Wire racer – until that is you notice the four round headlamps and the parking lamps. Mark III GT40M3/1106 belongs to Thomas Mittler.

Top

Thomas Mittler has two GT40s – and both of them are Mark IIIs. This one is the gleaming 1104, sitting outside its trailer at Road America.

Above

Halibrand wheels helped to turn the GT40 into a race winner, for the wire wheels which preceded them were incapable of withstanding the stresses imposed by (then) modern sticky tyres. They look good, too, as XGT-3 demonstrates.

Above

*Dale Nichols' Mark II was a team spare which never raced in
the sixties, although it is very active in vintage racing. A
mechanic who had worked on Shelby team cars back in those
halcyon days stopped in front of 427-powered XGT-3, parked
up at Road America, and his face broke into a wide grin. "I tell
people", he said, "there's one Mark II here which is just like I
remember them – this one!" It was easy to see what he
meant. XGT-3 has its share of minor blemishes, and the gener-
al patina of a car which isn't concours – it's a <u>race</u> car!*

Right

*When the opportunity arises to photograph a Mark IV chassis,
you take it. This is George Stauffer's J-4, the 1967 Sebring winner, being restored at his Blue Mounds premises in 1991. The
honeycomb aluminium tub is quite different from the GT40's
all-steel chassis. Note that in the roof are the two hinge points
for the forward tilting engine cover. For Le Mans 1967 this feature was changed in favour of a rear hinged lid, which on J-5
blew off and was almost destroyed.*

Opposite

*Now you know where the world's stock of the unique
J-car/Mark IV "turbine" wheels has gone. In the background is
J-4, in the throes of restoration.*

Above

The Henry Ford Museum generously permitted 1967 Le Mans winner J-6 to be present at the Road America gathering. This is another car which looks delightfully well-used. At one stage during the photo session the car was surrounded by spectators, but as all other cars were gradually removed, J-6 was left sitting there with only a handful of people around it. More than one of them wondered how he could sneak it out unnoticed!

Right

Shelby's Mark IVs were different from Holman & Moody's in lots of minor ways. For example, Shelby's cars had sliding side window openings, whilst Holman & Moody's had hinged ones. J-6 gave the USA its first (and only) all-American win at Le Mans, with Dan Gurney and A J Foyt setting new distance and speed records in the process.

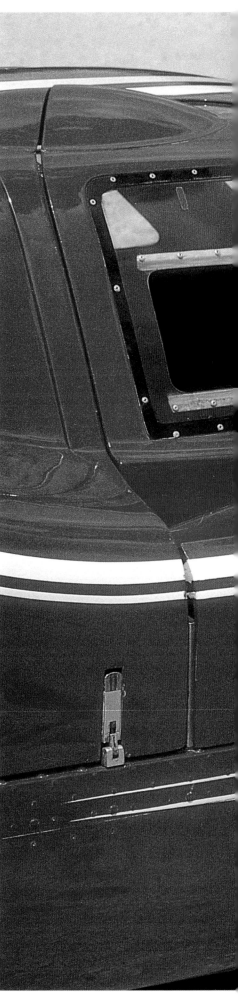

Right

It looks like the Le Mans winner, but it isn't. J-11 is the penultimate Mark IV, which J Arthur Urciuoli brought to Road America. At the front it has the brake ducts which were used only at Sebring 1967, and which were covered over on that year's Le Mans cars.

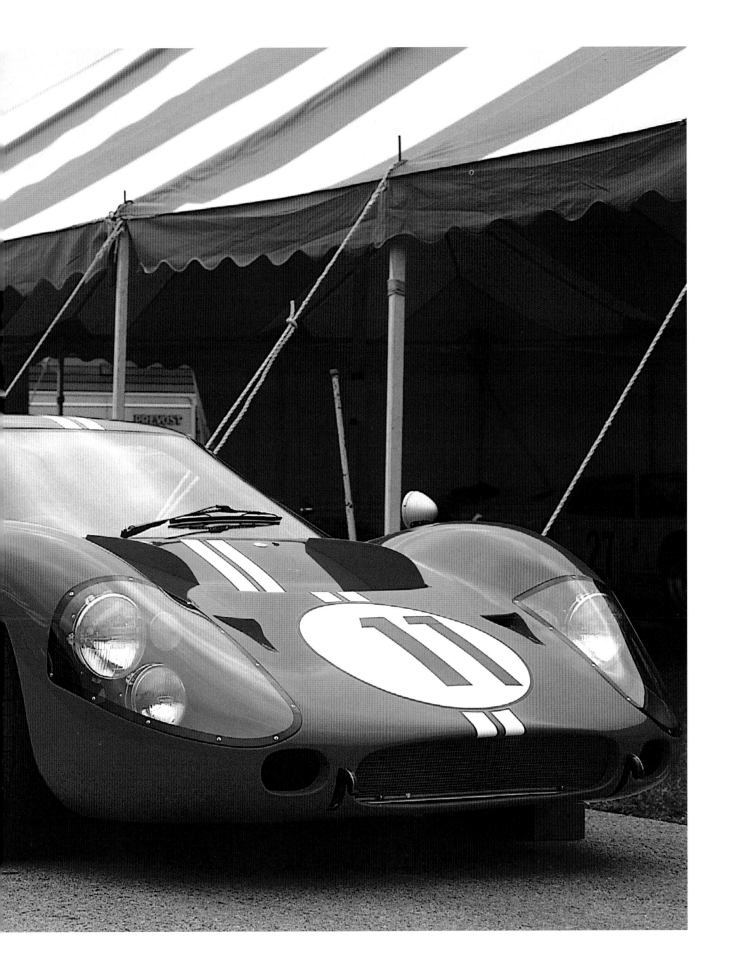

Above

Last of the Mark IVs, Rod Leach's J-12, at Silverstone in 1991. Not until 1994 did this car find its way back to the USA, to a new home in Phoenix.

Above right

This interesting car is "1047", built up by Bryan Wingfield with parts from many sources. The chassis was built using some pieces salvaged from an original, unidentified, GT40, some unused Abbey Panels parts (which were still in their protective green lacquer finish), and some new pieces from Tennant Panels. Thus, there's a lot of original GT40 in there. It was given its 1047 number because a plate bearing that number happened to be available. Incidentally, the original 1047, long thought to be the Ford France car which won the Reims 12-hour race, is instead almost certainly the "1031" which is with a Japanese owner who currently wishes to remain anonymous. Confusing, no?

Right

Peter Thorp (left) demonstrates just how light is the first of the alloy chassis he has built for Safir Engineering's officially sanctioned Mark V GT40s. There are only one or two left of the final production run, so buy now whilst stocks last.

Overleaf

ERA is now into big block cars, this being their first example, photographed outside their Connecticut workshops. The rear bodywork of this beautifully finished car was made from a mould taken from a body panel which had at one time graced 1046, so it ought to be accurate.

Above

106WR – the letters stand for Wingfield
Racing – was built by Bryan on a Sbarro
chassis. Unlike 1085A, the car was delivered as a bare tub, and was then built
up purely as a big-block racer, also for
René Herzog. It is seen here at the
Nürburgring. (Photo: Jürgen Strehle)

Left

Bryan Wingfield's first foray into GT40-
building (as opposed to restoration) was
Tennant Panels-chassised 1000BW, seen
here at Silverstone in 1990.

Below

Time to go home – 106WR is lifted into a truck for the journey home from Silverstone. 106WR has lighter body panels than 1085A, and it weighs in at around 2650 pounds. When tested by engine-builders Mathwall, the car's 427 engine produced the most torque they had ever seen from an engine that size – over 600lbsft!

Overleaf

This is the first example of the Mark V to be fitted with a big-block engine, and a tail bearing some of the Mark II's typical features. When road-tested by a US magazine, the 8-litre Mark V produced absolutely staggering performance figures – and at a cost that is a fraction of what has to be paid for a modern "supercar". (Photo: Pete Lyons)

Specifications

	1965 GT40	1966 Mark II-A	1967 Mark IV	1968 Mark III
Semi-monocoque chassis	Steel	Steel	Aluminium	Steel
Wheelbase, in inches	95	95	95	95
Dimensions, in inches				
Width	70	70	70.5	70
Length	164.5	163	171	169
Height	40.5	40.5	38.6	41
Weight				
With fuel and water, in pounds	2450	2700	2600	2600
Engine (iron block) V8				
Size in cubic centimetres	4736	6982	6982	4942
Size in cubic inches	289	427	427	302
Power, bhp	390	485	500	300
(at rpm)	7000	6200	6400	6000
Carburation	4 Weber	1 Holley	2 Holley	1 Holley
Gearbox, synchromesh	ZF	Ford	Ford	ZF
	5-speed	4-speed	4-speed	5-speed
Bodywork materials				
Front: Fibreglass, all models				
Rear: Fibreglass, all models				
Centre	Steel	Steel	Aluminium	Steel
Wheels	Alloy	Alloy	Alloy	Wire

Previous page and below

Latest of the modern production GT40s, Lee Holman's superb Mark II deserves to succeed; it's expensive of course, but it's so near perfect that if you can afford the asking price, it's worth every penny. (Photo: Pete Lyons)

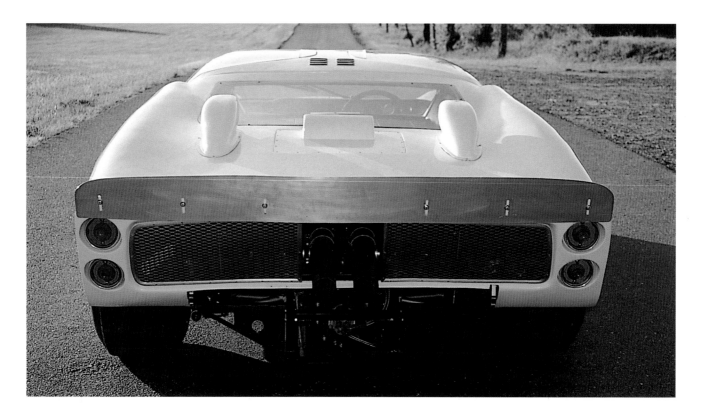